This Little Tiger book belongs to:

_____

_____

_____

For Mark, Anna and Charlotte
with my love – T C

To Laura, Grace and Oscar
for putting up with Trolls in the house
– L W

Daily Mail

LITTLE TIGER PRESS LTD,
an imprint of the Little Tiger Group
1 Coda Studios, 189 Munster Road, London SW6 6AW
www.littletiger.co.uk
First published in Great Britain 2010
This edition published 2016

A CIP catalogue record for this book is available
from the British Library • All rights reserved
ISBN 978-1-84869-495-8 • Printed in China
LTP/1800/3609/0920
10 9 8 7 6 5 4 3

Mouldy
wet Big
Bogeys

Tracey Corderoy

Lee Wildish

LITTLE TIGER
LONDON

THE GRUNT AND THE GROUCH

The Grunt was probably
the grumpiest troll you'd ever be
likely to meet. Just look at his face!
Now tell me – would you invite *him* to your
party? Well, one day someone did just that.
And things were never quite the same again . . .

It happened on a Tuesday – the most *boring* day of the week –
this scrappy bit of paper landed on The Grunt's dirty doormat . . .
"What's **this?**" he cried, snatching it up.
So he read the scruffy writing . . .

KEEP
OUT!

"Who's **dared** leave this on my mat?"
growled The Grunt.
"I **don't** like Tuesdays. I **don't** like visitors.
And I **really don't** like parties . . .
so I'm not coming!"

With that, he tore the invitation into
tiny shreds, then stomped back inside
and finally got to work . . .

Not picking bits of mould off his teeth . . .

Not cleaning the bath . . .

Not doing the washing up . . .

Not even flushing the toilet!

Boring Tuesday morning ended and boring Tuesday afternoon began. So The Grunt went to town — it was, after all, the perfect place . . .

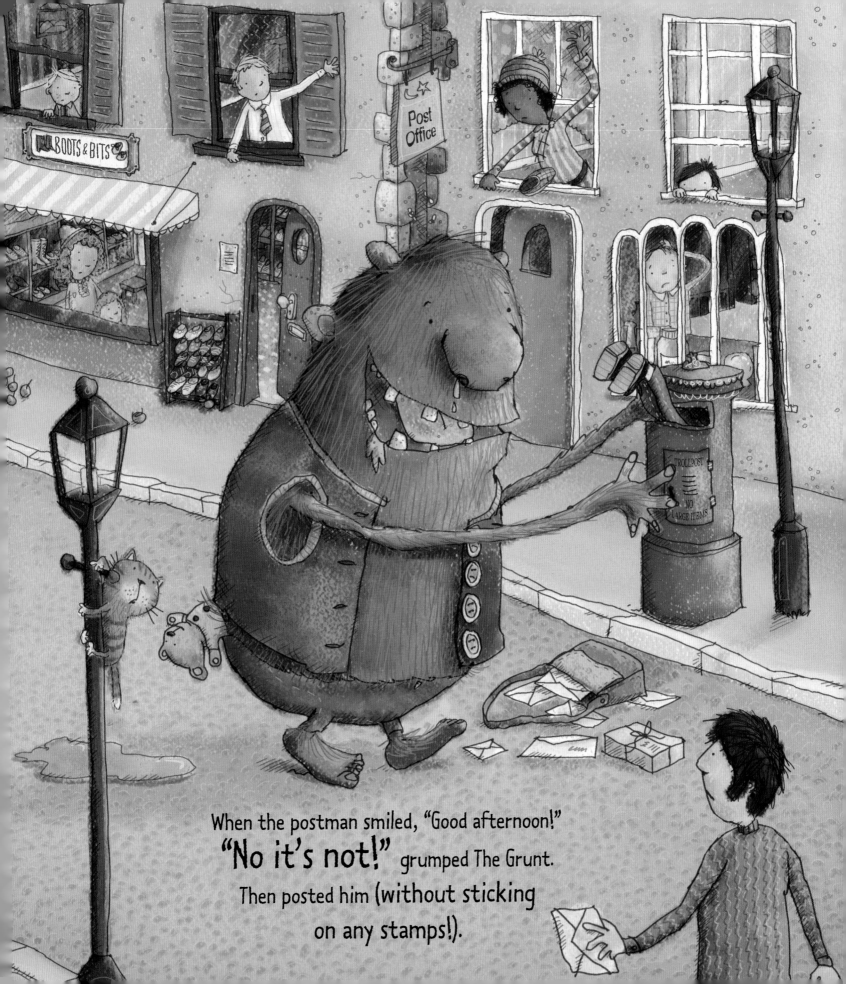

When the postman smiled, "Good afternoon!"
"No it's not!" grumped The Grunt.
Then posted him (without sticking
on any stamps!).

Back home, as The Grunt thundered in through his gate, who should he find but **a visitor!**

"**Grrrrrr!**" he bellowed. "I'm The Grunt! No one parties in **my** garden!"

HOME SWEET HOME

WET WORMS

Bang! Bang! Bang!

He waved a dirty fingernail.
"Now clear off!" he snarled.
Then **bang – bang – bang** went the pretty balloons
as The Grunt popped every one!

"Oi – party pooper!" snapped The Grouch.
"You great big grunty grump!"
Then he chucked a chunk of
his pongiest cheese . . .

And that's when the food

fight began.

"Hang on a minute . . ." said The Grunt.
"Those maggot-cakes look **great!**"
So they sat and ate and The Grunt had such fun
he forgot to be mean . . . he forgot to be *bored* and
he *even* forgot to send The Grouch away!

"Now . . ." burped The Grunt.
"What else can we do?"

"Troll stuff!" cried The Grouch.

So they messed around
with spots and goo . . .

took turns to **cheat** at
a game or two . . .

and hid from the sunshine . . .
together!

A whole week later, The Grouch packed up his tent.
"Oh well, Grunty," he sighed. "It's been great!
But now I must go. See – I always
move garden on a Tuesday . . ."

Keep OUT!

"But . . . *why?*" said The Grunt. And then he saw it —
the tiny troll looked . . . *sad.* The Grunt had never
seen sad before. What's more, he'd never cared!
But now . . . suddenly . . . he did.

"You asked me why I go," said The Grouch,
    disappearing through the gate. "I go because . . .
no one's ever asked me to stay."

But where was The Grouch?
He'd disappeared! So The Grunt
searched high and low.

He raced. He chased.
He dashed. He crashed!

And then, at last . . .

...he found him!

"Grouchy – stay!" panted The Grunt.

"Wow – thanks . . ." sniffed the little Grouch.

Then The Grunt felt his lips go all tickly
and begin to curl up to his ears . . .
"What's this?" he said. It felt *so good!*
And The Grouch cried, "I think we're **smiling!**"

But, every Tuesday, they get dressed up.
Now it's their **favourite** day!
For that's the day . . .

Jane Hissey

Happy Birthday
Old Bear